Three spotty monsters
up in a balloon.

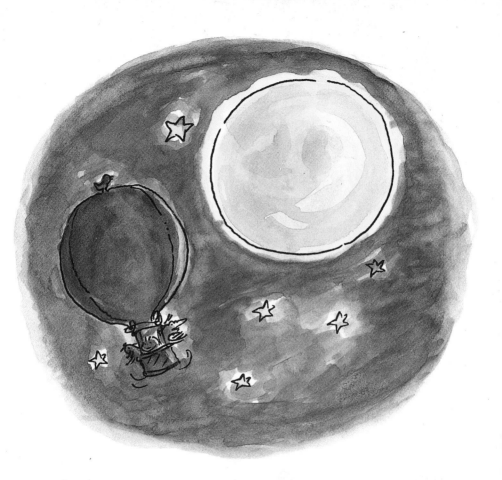

Three spotty monsters
flying to the moon.

Three spotty monsters
waving to a train.

Three spotty monsters
waving to a plane.

Three spotty monsters
waving to the stars.

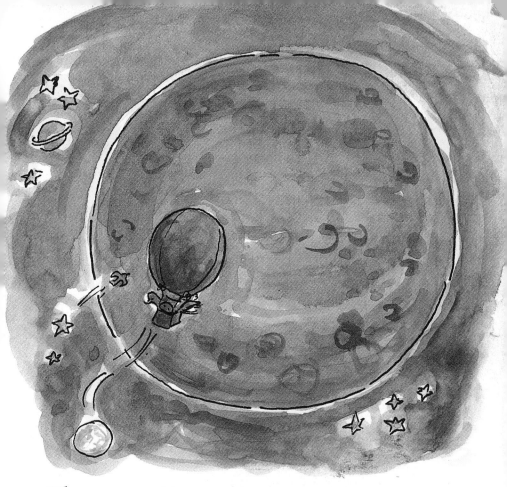

Three spotty monsters
flying off to Mars.